DISCLAIMER

Whilst every effort has been made to ensure accuracy of production, no responsibility can be accepted for any actions that may be taken or advice given by persons reading this book. No litigation will be entered into by the author in any circumstances, without prejudice.

CONTENTS

FIGURES

JOHN HARRISON- BIOGRAPHY OF A PALMIST

Born in West London, John possessed the "intuitive gifts" since childhood, of clairvoyance, clairsentience and visions. Being naturally creative he wrote poetry from an early age, and later short stories and songs. Although not academically bright, due to dyslexia, he studied English, Religion, Law and Politics and chose to go into retail and sales management, as his first career path.

However, John's main interest was in Religion. In his teenage years he studied Astrology and Palmistry, and began practicing Yoga, Meditation and Tai Chi Chan, being fascinated by Daoism and Hinduism. This found fruition, when he became the Chairman of the Theosophical Society [Alcott Lodge], organising and attending lectures by the leading religious authorities of those days. He also lectured himself, having written his Thesis on Palmistry Counselling, the profession he was to found.

Not content to just be a student, having experienced a "Samadhi", John began a lifelong Quest to discover the truth of being, and the Path to Self-Realisation and Spiritual Enlightenment. He learnt that in all the major religions there were references to the Word of God, [sound vibrations], and Knowledge of God [Light frequencies].Whilst this philosophy was intellectually appealing, the Mind never becomes enlightened.

So began the search for a Perfect Master, who could reveal by their Grace, the Truth of Being. Having participated in a whole succession of "spiritual paths", where teachers purported to take the aspirant on a journey to enlightenment, but failed to mention that they, they were NOT enlightened, many illusions were experienced! However, fortunately in 2004, at last found a genuine Path, with a Perfect Master and joined The Path of Light and Sound, where he hoped to complete his journey to Liberation, during this life!

On the work front, regrettably subsequent to recession and austerity, John's family retail business reached its nemesis in 1988, when his parents Alan and Joyce retired. Unemployed for the first time in years, he took this opportunity to travel around the world, experiencing many diverse cultures, revelling in their traditions and spiritual ceremonies. Upon return, began to train as an Aroma therapist and Spiritual Healer, going on to become a psychotherapist, hypnotherapist, Seichem Tera Mai Healing Master, as well as studying Tanta and Chi Kung. With this experience, started the Smile Holistic Practice.

In 1989, whilst travelling in India was involved in a major road traffic accident, but miraculously escaped virtually unscathed. Upon returning to England, sought treatment at a local Mind, Body and Soul Exhibition. It was a wonderful experience, and found out then, that such Exhibitions occurred all over the country, where Tarot Readers, Clairvoyants and Palmists could earn a living by giving Readings to an appreciative public.

Over successive years, he has been published in leading magazines, as well as appeared on national T.V. and radio, given lectures on Palmistry Counselling in the U.S.A. where my exemplary knowledge and experience dispelled many of the myths about Palmistry, and I was accorded great respect, by their teachers, who sent their students to purchase his home tuition palmistry counselling manuals, and have readings!

Palmistry Counselling is the new career that he has established. It is a collaboration of the skills of Hand Analysis [Chirology], married to the Art of Hand Divination [Palmistry], which is rooted in the philosophy of Alchemy, Metaphysical Heurism and Ontology, and the psychological insights of the counsellor. Palmistry Counselling is a therapeutic discipline, aimed at empowering clients to attain their full potential in heath, careers and relationships.

In conclusion, Palmistry Counselling is a practical discipline offering insights into our purpose in life. For those seeking answers to questions, a good grounding in metaphysics and philosophy is necessary. Then beyond palmistry, can be found the Path to Self-Realisation and Enlightenment.

For private readings, party bookings, exhibition or corporate events, articles, lectures, T.V or Radio Appearances, or to learn Palmistry Counselling contact John Harrison at his Web-site;-

www.john-harrison-palmistry.com

SMILE HOLISTIC PRACTICE

Meditation and Personal Development

To learn to relax, release stress, find peace, serenity, balance and equanimity, or to go on the journey leading to self- realisation and spiritual enlightenment, visit my Web-site:-

www.meditation-4u2.com

DAO CHI KUNG FOUNDATION

"The Way to Do is to Be."

Breath is Life,

Life is Well Being

*Beginners Course in Chi Kung

[Breathe, Stand, Store Chi Energy]

*Intermediate Course in Chi Kung

[Meditation-The Inner Smile]

* Advanced Course in Chi Kung

[Practice-Healing Sounds]

To learn Chi Kung,

Attend a Free Talk,

Book a Class, or

Attend a Workshop

Contact John Harrison [Dip Chi Kung]

www.smileholistictherapies.com

E Mail:- smile4u2024@yahoo.co.uk

Seichem Tera Mai Healing Courses and Treatments

Learn to rejuvenate, re-energise, and heal yourself or others. One to one sessions, healing courses/work shops available from this experienced Seichem Master.

Palmistry COUNSELLING by John Harrison, one of U.K.'s leading Palmists!

Follow Me on Social Media at

https://www.facebook.com/people/John-Harrison/1784112544

https://twitter.com/palmistryjohn

INTRODUCTION TO PALMISTRY COUNSELLING?

Palmistry Counselling is a wonderful form of guidance and advice, because it covers all areas of your life in great detail and offers an interpretation of your life purpose!. So, whether you are interested in your health, career, relationship, or the more in depth issues of psychology, philosophy or spirituality, palmistry counselling provides the answers. Of particular importance is the fact that a Reading covers the whole of your life, rather than just the next few years.

This is an ancient discipline, originating in the Sacred Sanskrit Texts, of the Indian Sub-Continent called The Vedas ,thought to have been conceived thousands of years ago. Strongly associated with Astrology, Aristotle brought it to the West, and Chiromancy [Hand Magic],was consulted by great men and women throughout history such as Napolean Bonaparte.

WHAT CAN PALMISTRY COUNSELLING DO FOR YOU?

In short it can provide you with the ANSWERS ,so you can solve your own problems! Palmistry counselling is a modern profession created by John HARRISON.
It draws upon Astrological Symbolism, such as the meanings of the Planets and Stars[known to you through your Birth Chart],and the Elements, Earth ,Air, Fire and Water. Every good Palmist should be knowledgeable concerning the Science of Chirology [Hand Analysis], which is the basis for interpreting the hands.

But palmistry counselling is so much more than just the ability to assess character, personality, profession or romantic orientation, for when we apply intuition, psychic insight and a working knowledge of psychology, then the counselling and empowerment for you to change your life for the better, comes into its own element. The result is to give you a deep, meaningful and comprehensive framework for living your life productively, thereby transforming your attitudes to work ,maintenance of your health in harmony with nature, and how to be happier in all your relationships. The reason for this, in a nutshell, is rather than just receiving a one off interpretation of what's happening now, or what are the future trends, you yourself are given the tools to influence your own destiny, and the power to transform your whole approach to life, and make it more likely to attain health, wealth and happiness.

SO , WHAT ARE YOUR QUESTIONS?

Do you need to know what you need to do to improve your health?
Or ,perhaps help you to recover from a complaint?
Are you aware that prominent physicians, such as Dr Charlotte Wolfe, and Doctor Benham used to diagnose illnesses, by consulting the hands up until modern times?

HOW CAN YOU IMPROVE YOUR HEALTH

Are you in need of advice about your health?
What do your Hands tell you about your present life-style?
Do you need to address your addictions ie drinking, smoking etc
How long will you live?
What can you do to live a vibrant, healthy life?

Relationships in love can also be discerned.

ARE YOU COMPATIBLE WITH YOUR PARTNER?

Are your characters and personalities complimentary or antagonistic?
Do you see yourself getting married , having children, finding love and happiness?
And how will you relate to your children?
Will you stay together, separate, or will you get back together with a lost lover?

WHAT CAREER PATH SHOULD YOU CHOOSE?

Are you out of work, and seeking a new career direction?
Have you moved house to a different location, and wondering if you will find a suitable job?
Perhaps your career is in the doldrums, and you are seeking fresh start?
Would it be best for you to be self -employed, gain more qualifications or chose a new profession?
Are you better suited to a vocation, such as teaching, nursing or working for a charity?
Finally, maybe you have decided to give up work to nurture children or go travelling?

Palmistry holds the answers to these questions, and also the larger picture ,such as the actual purpose of your life, what you are here for, and what you can do to transform your life!!!

HOW CAN PALMISTRY COUNSELLING TELL YOU ALL THIS?

According to Astrology, the positions of the Planets and Stars affect our lives.
And the Elements in a Chart, are significant in your personal life.
Does this all sound a bit irrational , or superstitious?
Well, No, not really!!!
We are know that the Moon affects our moods, women's menstrual cycles and the weather!
The Sun similarly regulates our climate, from growing crops to drought.
So, it is quite plausible that the Planets such as Jupiter, Saturn as well as the more distant
Stars have a subtle, but important role to play in our lives. The reason for this at a deep
level is that everything in the Universe is connected by a stream of energy , like waves or
currents that ebb and flow, that create harmony or conflict. When we "go with the flow",
all goes well in our life, but when we swim against the tide, troubles arise. So   sometimes
it's best to "sit tight" and wait, whilst other times we should surge forward optimistically.
The trick is to find out when are the most auspicious times for growth, but when we should
hold back and wait.

Fortunately, palmistry counselling enables us to learn these important lessons in safety and
security, so that we become wiser and in control of our lives.

WHY PALMISTRY COUNSELLING WORKS.......LIKE MAGIC?

There are 3 Categories within **Palmistry**.

Chirognomy-The Shape of the Hands[your character and personality]
Chiromancy- The Features of the Palms ie Lines.[your Map of Life; or direction]
Dermatoglyphics-The Finger Prints and Skin Ridge Patterns.[your mental and social
conditioning; or cultural setting]

CHIROGNOMY-THE HAND SHAPES

From the 4 Different Hand Shapes, we can determine;
*Your Health, Stamina, Energy and potential longevity
*Your Psychology ,Philosophy ,interest in Religion or Politics.
*Through Hand Shape Synastry how you will relate to Partners or your children ie
Compatability.
*The best range of careers suited to you, and why this is so!

CHIROMANCY-THE MAP OF YOUR LIFE.

Looking at your hands, you may notice that there are probably lots of lines and bumps and and the texture of the skin may be rough or smooth? Well to the experienced palmistry counsellor this is like a Map, that can be read, determining what direction you may choose to take in life ie a Journey. But also, what route NOT to take, and why! So, it's easy, isn't it-Take the right road and end up at your destination OR take the wrong highway, and end up lost, or in trouble ie a road block or cliff!

EXAMPLES OF WHY THIS IS TRUE!

The Life Line indicates your general physical health, and life force energy , or endurance.
The Heart Line shows your emotional response to life , feelings and romantic inclinations.
The Head Line indicates your psychology ie thoughtful or impetuous; logical or imaginative.
The Fate Line shows your Life Purpose, your vocation and faith , and how Events unfold.
The Sun Line [Apollo] indicates creativity and public service Fame and Fortune.
There are many other less prominent, but still important lines, of which the most misinterpreted by amateurs must be the Marriage and Children Lines, which provide potential for happiness. Fortunately the palmistry counsellor can not only analyse these lines, under the Little Finger, but apply psychic insight and therapeutic skills to assist you!

DERMATOGLYPHICS- INHERITED GENETIC CONDITIONING.

The Fingerprints and Skin Ridge Patterns are the most fascinating area of .
From a medical perspective they represent our parents chromosomes, being genetic features.

FINGERPRINTS

Whereas the Fingers in general represent our Mental Landscape and Psychology, the Finger Print Patterns represent our Individuality, and finely tuned beliefs, and cultural perspectives
Therefore, for example they can indicate;
• Whether you are emotional, imaginative, flexible and adaptable.
• However, are you more fixed, individualistic, unorthodox and freedom loving?

• Or perhaps practical, good at business, or making crafts?
• Possibly highly strung ,energetic ,nervous, or obsessed?
All these mental characteristics make up who you are, what you think, and how you see the World, but are they fixed, or can they be changed?

The skin ridge patterns can determine:-
*Your sense of humour
* Whether you are serious and committed in your beliefs
*If you are a born leader
* Or brave, courageous, or psychic?

IN CONCLUSION

Palmistry Counselling enables you to ask the right questions,
Receive the right answers for your own individual needs.
Apply them constructively to your circumstances and you can
find your purpose in life and be in harmony with the Heavens.

You have the whole world in your hands, so by learning the fascinating art of palmistry counselling you can apply this knowledge to change your life for the better!

THE KEYS TO YOUR PALMISTRY STUDIES!

Anyone who decides to take a trip, let's say to visit another country, will need good advice. There are so many things to think of and if you're not careful you'll find yourself at the airport without some important document, your jewellery, maybe a hat or sun-screen cream! Like a vacation, in order to enjoy palmistry you'll need a list of items so that when that wonderful moment arrives, when someone shows you their hands, you won't be confused.

'The Keys to Palmistry' is such a list. But before we explore these tools we need to remember that with palmistry we are dealing with people and so diplomacy and compassion are needed. Imagine what it would be like if you went to a book store and the sales assistant was rude and bad tempered – would you make a purchase there? No! So, even if someone asks you to look at their hands and appears casual or joking, never forget the privilege, responsibility and duty you have been given – to tell the truth but be tactful. Never underestimate the power of the spoken word to help or to injure. Remember also that we are all human and like to hear good news, so be positive and have a concerned attitude.

Now, the first lesson to be learnt in palmistry is that every part of the hand has individual characteristics that can be interpreted according to the laws of Chirology. From a spiritual point of view the hand represents consciousness, showing the journey of our souls in this life-time. Psychologically the hand represents our dreams, desires and motivations, both through our mental and emotional experiences. Physically the hand represents our bodies and what we do with them, e.g. swimming, jogging, dancing, fighting, making love, eating, drinking and many more activities. So the hands help us to know more about ourselves physically, psychologically and spiritually – who we are, where we are going and how we are going to get there. But such a map must have signs and symbols to guide us, and they do.

KEYWORD ASSOCIATIONS

THE SUN (APOLLO)

- Brilliance, creativity, communication, art, beauty, music, pleasure, public life, fame, adventure.

MERCURY

- Mental dexterity, ideology, intellect, inquisitiveness, mathematics, communications, fertility, medicine, skeletal and nervous systems.

VENUS

- Strength, passion, sensuality, love, vitality, parental influence, physical, health, food and drink.

MARS

- Temper, anger, resistance to illness, ambition, courage, assertiveness.

LOWER MARS

- Bravery, strength, stamina, risk-taking.

UPPER MARS

- Heroism, fortitude, aggression, charisma.

THE MOON

- Spirituality, sensitivity, intuition, psychic abilities, delusions, visions, attunement, contemplation, mental instability (lunacy).

EARTH

- Home, safety, physical stamina, conservation, family, cultures, societies.

JUPITER

- Pride, dignity, idealism, compassion, belief, inspiration, love, elation, confidence.

SATURN

- Tradition, severity, discipline, stability, administration, property, legal matters, careers, finance success.

URANUS

- Invention, business acumen, change, perception of time, metabolic health, genius, dynamic creativity or destruction.

NEPTUNE

- Fantasies, spirituality, mysticism, sensitivity, dreams and visions, imagination, delusions, foolishness.

PLUTO

- Secrecy, intensity, addictions, sensitivity, sexuality, transcendence, healing abilities, psychic experiences, psychology.

THE HISTORY OF HAND STUDIES

Since ancient times, our ancestors have looked up into the sky, marvelling at the beauty of the stars and planets. In recorded history, the Chaldeans, Assyrians, and Egyptians began the study of Astronomy and Astrology.

Like Astrology, in Palmistry one method of hand analysis involves planetary symbols. Under this system:

the THUMB is represented by the planet MARS:

the INDEX FINGER is ruled by JUPITER:

the SECOND or MIDDLE FINGER is said to be ruled by SATURN:

the THIRD or RING FINGER is assigned to the SUN (or APOLLO):

and the FOURTH or LITTLE FINGER is ruled by MERCURY.

These characteristics are also said to rule regions or areas of the hands, called the MOUNT, with an expanded planetary symbology taking in VENUS, NEPTUNE and two regions governed by MARS, i.e. UPPER MARS and LOWER MARS, as well as LUNA (Moon).

This system has evolved in Europe and was utilised by prominent men such as Aristotle and Augustus Caesar, but in later centuries were taken up by the Celts and the Romany Gypsies of Eastern Europe and Russia. By the process Palmistry became divided into two distinct and separate groups of people; the Gypsies who drew upon psychic powers and who were knowledgeable concerning herbalism and astrology and the men of science who distanced themselves from the Gypsies whom they deemed as charlatans. This latter group, following the earlier Greek teachings, called themselves Chirologists from the Greek word "Kheir" meaning 'hand' and "Ology" briefly described as "the logical study of".

The origins of Chirology are ancient, stemming from the Vedas, the Indian Sanskrit texts written 2000 years before Christ. Chirology evolved in India where it is still practiced in conjunction with Astrology and Ayuvedevic medicine. It also spread to China, where it became integrated over thousands of years into the Chinese Buddhist religion. Based upon the Elements of Earth, Air, Fire, Water and Ether as opposed to the Western planetary system, Eastern Chirology is profoundly complex, but in its simplest terms it is based upon the laws of Nature.

History often teaches us about the nature of conflict and Palmistry is no stranger to controversy. Many eminent Chirologists will not associate themselves with Palmistry, claiming that it is a profession governed by fakes, frauds, confidence tricksters or demented people being the "Art of Hand Divination" or Fortune Telling. Palmists on the other hand, maintain that they are seers, possessing intuitive gifts and can accurately predict the future. This viewpoint is ridiculed by the Chirologists who call themselves "Hand Analysts" and give guidance on health, career and relationship matters. They interpret but do not predict.

As a Palmistry counsellor I see the value of both Chirology and Palmistry, i.e. Analysis and intuition combined; and I teach the Western tradition of Chirology, this being the most easily evaluated by english speaking people, including our American, Canadian and Australian friends who share a similar educational system.

The Map of Your Life

PALMISTRY is the study of hands, which is the map of life. CHIROGNOMY represents the structure of your hands. Physically this is the metacarpal bones, the radial and ulnar arteries, the nerves, blood vessels and finally the skin and nails. From the psychological point of view there are four hand shapes, these being THE SQUARE or Practical Hand; THE SPATULATE or Energetic Hand; THE CONIC or Artistic Hand; and THE PHILOSPOPHICAL or Intellectual Hand.

CHIROMANCY represents the Palmar Regions, specifically the Major and Minor lines, their qualities and flow across your hand. Here we will examine depth, width, tone and definition. These are like rivers and streams showing your journeys.

Next we will look at THE MOUNTS (small mounds of flesh) which rise like mountains from the hand and represent your gifts or abilities.

DERMATOGLYPHICS represent the skin ridge patterns and your individual finger print patterns. On the finger tips they show psychological characteristics; on the palm they show aspects of your personality, e.g. humour, seriousness, memory, etc.

CHIROGNOMY –The Outer Form

Chirology, or Scientific Palmistry, comprises Chirognomy (the Shape of Hands) and Chiromancy (The Palmar Regions).

Physically, or from a physiological perspective, the human hand is composed of Metacarpal bones, the Radial and Ulnar arteries, peripheral blood vessels, nerve endings, the skin formation and nail structure. While Chirognomy is concerned with the structure and shape of the hands, Dermatoglyphics deal with skin ridge patterns, an example of which can be seen in the finger print records kept by the police.

CHIROMANCY – The Inner Form

Concerned with the Palmar Regions, the mounts and lines on the hand. The colour, texture and temperature of the skin metabolism, the width, depth, tone and definition of the lines give great insight into a person's abilities, their strengths and weaknesses. Chirognomy deals with the character of people, their outward consciousness of the world, whereas Chiromancy deals with their personality and psychology, the inner workings of their lives, career, relationships, health and chronology.

A person's left hand represents their origins, family, their potential and passive feminine strengths. It is also a record of their lives, similar to a library. A person's right hand represents their evolvement, will direction and orientation to the world; and a person's active masculine strengths. However, if your client is left handed these qualities are reversed.

Left handed people are imaginative, intuitive, perceptive. Often gifted in the fields of art and music, and in many athletics or physical agility is to be found. There are also many successful left handed business people.

Right handed people show reasoning abilities, logic, adaptability and the capacity to learn. Most people from Europe, Australia the USA and Canada are right handed.

HAND TYPE CLASSIFICATION   (Refer to Figure One)

A   SQUARE/PRACTICAL HANDS – "I Serve"

Description: Square palm with short fingers; thick, wide palms; coarse skin, few deep lines; square finger tips.

Key Words: Practical, reliable, conventional, trustworthy, loving food, the countryside. Traditional, distrustful of words. Cautious, reserved, seeking capable and down to earth partners, patient, tolerant, with excellent stamina. Sometimes reserved, often useful with their hands, e.g. craft-work, tool-making.

Career Orientations: Farming, engineering, building, horticulture, cooking, mining, sculpture, dancing, athletics (weight-lifting, boxing)

B   CONIC/EMOTIONAL HANDS - "I Feel"

Description: Oblong palm with narrow, tapering fingers; long, thin, narrow or rounded palms; fine skin; soft, elastic fingers; pointed tips.

Key Words: Sensitive, artistic, sympathetic, responsive, compassionate, emotional, fastidious, spiritual, versatile, fertile, musical.

Career Orientations: Nurses, doctors, artists, musicians, actors, nuns, athletics (swimming, running), counsellors, therapists, linguists.

C   PHILOSOPHICAL/MENTAL HANDS – "I Think"

Description: Square palm with long wide fingers. Short, wide palms; dry, fine skin; long broad fingers; rounded tips.

Key Words: Thoughtful, intellectual, unconventional, humorous, inventive, logical, impersonal, perceptive, quick witted, diplomatic, critical.

Career Orientations: Scholars, diplomats, doctors, lawyers, politicians broadcasters, entertainers, directors, teachers, inventors, professors, religious leaders.

D   SPATULATE/ENERGETIC HANDS - "I Act"

Description: Oblong palm with short fingers; long, wide, thick palms; elastic, springy skin; short, spatulate fingers.

Key Words: Energetic, active, intuitive, impetuous, creative, enthusiastic, argumentative, inspired, restless, unconventional – The Pioneer.

Career Orientations: Soldiers, explorers, astronauts, engineers, authors, seers, chefs, pilots, travel couriers, sales managers, leaders in business & industry.

FIGURE ONE: HAND TYPE CLASSIFICATION

Philosophical Hands - Air
"I Think"

Spatulate Hands - Fire
"I Act"

Conic Hands - Water
"I Feel"

Square Hands - Earth
"I Serve"

THE FINGERS AND THUMBS

Fingers represent our spheres of interests and our grasp of the Real World. They indicate our intellectual attributes and our conscious desires for self expression. The fingers are ruled by Planets as follows:

THUMB = MARS- Logic, Willpower and Direction in life

INDEX FINGER = JUPITER- Inspirations, Ambition, Creativity, Ego, Food & Money

MIDDLE FINGER = SATURN- Traditions, Science, Law, Ethics, Religious Institutions, Agriculture and Craftsmanship

RING FINGER = APOLLO- Music, Sports, Arts, Self-expression, Public offices

LITTLE FINGER = MERCURY- Communications, Electronics, Linguistics, Medicine, Sexuality and Children

THE THUMB – ETHER

In Palmistry the Thumb expresses the Energy of the Individual. In direct terms it represents a person's willpower, decision-making abilities and passions.

There are three settings for the Thumb – lower, medial and high. The lower example indicates a person of strength, who has physical agility and may be drawn to sporting activities. The medial position is a balanced one, illustrating a sense of harmony between physical and mental pursuits. The higher setting is that of the aspirant, one who is idealistic and pursues intellectual stimulation. They may enjoy discussing art or music, or be attracted to the professions. However they may be narrow minded and dogmatic.

There is great debate as to the ideal length of this digit. I ascertain that each phalange should be equal in length, indicating a balanced reasoning ability and the correct application of judgement, resulting in organisation.

The first or lower phalange of the thumb represents desire to create, the desire to act. This area is termed the Mount of Venus.

The second phalange shows reasoning ability. When full and waited this indicated diplomacy, tact and a desire to maximise the economy of energy expended. When over-long, this section causes the subject to be indecisive and to prefer to argue and debate matters, being incapable of acting. A short phalange shows that the person will be impulsive, instinctively acting sometimes without any clear cut plan. A thick, wide middle phalange indicates an honest, direct approach to others. Diplomacy may be lacking! This person may deliberate rather than act and is not easily counselled.

The third phalange relates to the "fuel" of power divested in the thumb and thus refers to action. A long phalange herein tells of the subject's great determination, stamina and persistence. Thin, long phalanges indicate subtlety and great precision – an eye surgeon could have such a thumb to enhance the accuracy and deftness their profession requires of them.

Very thin nail phalanges show the strategist, one who succeeds with apparently little effort.

Square tipped thumbs are practical and often found on the palms of engineers. There is also present a love of the truth and an inherent desire for justice.

Spatulate thumbs are the tool of the craftsman – painters, sculptors and musicians often have this formation.

Clubbed thumbs used to be considered to indicate a confused of frustrated nature. In past times called "The Murderers' Thumb", such melodramatic terminology is inappropriate and misleading. The true meaning is that these people are deficient in the actuation of this willpower at an instinctive level. Whilst this may also be true of criminals, I have met many charming and capable people with this feature! However, I believe this means hardship and inner turmoil. People with such formations often lack willpower and may be drawn towards deviancy or perversion. Once I found this sign on the hand of a charming man who excelled in professional career but unfortunately involved himself in pornography and child molesting. However this is not always the case and when found only on the left hand may only indicate an obsessive and obtuse individual.

Note the flexibility of the joints. Great flexibility of the thumb tip is a certain indication of the spend-thrift or gambler and shows a lack is of perseverance. However such individuals quickly adapt to the changing circumstances of home and career. A fixed joint indicates stubbornness.

Finally note if the upper phalange is held into the palm or curves outwards. A curved phalange indicates a generous nature, one who gives to others and may take up a cause on their behalf. A close-held thumb indicates a self-indulgent nature but may also be interpreted as cautious or reserved.

INDEX-FINGER – JUPITER

Representing ego and self awareness; our desire to express ourselves, expand our abilities, to exhibit our talents.

This finger should reach to the bottom of the nail of the Middle Finger. People with longer fingers attain to positions of leadership, e.g. directors, professors or university teachers.

A short finger indicates lack of confidence and the inability to assert will- power. When the top phalange is short a marked sense of inferiority may be present.

The lower Jupiterian phalange, when full, illustrates a person who likes good food and material luxuries. Such a person is independent but is sensitive to their environment – they like to choose their conditions of work. Short, narrow phalanges indicate hardships, perhaps poverty or a repressed childhood. A good second phalange shows the ability to organise; a man may be a D.I.Y enthusiast, a woman may have excellent secretarial or managerial abilities. Often men with large phalanges have business abilities or an aptitude for accounts or economics. When short, a person may not make the best of their opportunities or remain in a subordinate position. A long upper phalange indicates nobility, idealism and aspiration and is the hallmark of a person in authority. Diplomats, Politicians and Religious leaders often have such a phalange. However, when rounded, dominance and an overbearing nature may be apparent.

The finger should be straight. When bent inward onto the second finger this indicates sacrifices to cause, or loyalty to family ties.

SECOND FINGER – SATURN

This finger in its highest form represents science, law, philosophy (especially morality) and administration. Generally it shows how a person relates to society and responsibilities and is intimately concerned with career prospects and social position. It is ruled by Saturn the Stabiliser.

An overly long finger indicates a reserved and studious individual, perhaps over-cautious, but responsible. Narrow mindedness may prevail. Short fingers indicate a rebellious nature or a person unable to settle down. Extremely short fingers are the hallmark of the professional criminal.

Long base phalanges indicate gifts in crafts, botany, farming or archaeology. The strong second phalange indicates executive ability, being the hallmark of the lawyer, doctor and those who achieve management positions in private or public offices.

A short middle phalange shows impatience, irresponsibility and a lack of interest in attaining to positions of authority. A well-proportioned nail phalange indicates intellectual ability in the fields of law, science and art – however this person will demand respect and may not be modest about their attributes.

A straight finger shows self-restraint and a poised person. If found leaning towards Apollo (ring finger), job satisfaction and not financial reward is the primary career motive.

A square tip to this finger is preferable, depicting instinctive, practical judgement.

A flexible nail phalange indicates intuitive or psychic abilities; if the whole finger is flexible a person may be gullible or self-deceptive. Where the top finger joint is knotted, i.e. bulges out, this is the sign of the philosopher, deep thinker and writer!

THIRD FINGER – APOLLO

This finger represents creative expression and an emotional motivation towards happiness. Apollo was the Sun God and bestowed musical and artistic gifts upon followers. Whereas the index finger relates to private ambitions, the third finger relates to public life. In my experience, a long finger is the hallmark of the moral person, being a sign of perfectionism, bestowing gifts of oratory (as on the hands of teachers and salespeople) of creative gifts (as on the hands of artists, musicians and dancers).

The top of the finger should be level with the middle of the upper phalange of Suture (middle finger). A short finger shows an adventurous soul, a pioneer or gambler.

A long base phalange shows a competent gardener or decorator or possibly a sculptor and maybe a painter or musician. A short phalange indicates frustrations, lack of comfort or a detrimental environment. A long middle phalange shows selectivity of creative pursuits – the specialist. A precision tool-maker or fashion designer may have this formation; they use economy and like objects to be functional. A long nail phalange is the sign of the art historian, composer or graphic designer. They appreciate the exactness of colour, tone or the importance of a correct brush stroke.

Apollo fingers should be straight. When they lean towards Saturn (middle finger) this indicates a sense of duty and such people may be anxious to please parents. A square tip to the nail phalange shows a good eye for proportions. A knotted second joint indicates a tidy person with a love of order. An overly long finger indicates perfectionism – the sign of a critic.

FOURTH FINGER –MERCURY

In proportion, this finger should come half way up to the nail phalange of the Apollo finger (ring finger). Long fingers show personal charisma, sex appeal and excellent power of oratory or the capacity for abstract thought. A short finger denotes quick wittedness and sudden temper.

The base phalange rules money. A thick phalange indicates a desire to collect. Long second phalanges are the mark of the accountant, linguist or scientist (perhaps a doctor). Short second phalanges are symptoms of confusion of spendthrift nature. A good nail phalange shows gifts of speech and an intuitive understanding of others.

However, when long and bent towards Apollo a person may deceive; when curved towards the palm indicates a business person or a talent for theft.

A wide angled finger of Mercury indicates independence and an outspoken nature. Close held fingers are traditional or modest. A low set finger indicates difficulties in childhood and such people hate criticism and tend to be cautious in words and action. Often "dropped" little fingers show immaturity and naïveté. However, on a positive note, these people often get on well with children and animals because they are playful and sensitive. Flexible fingers show a retentive memory.

SPACING BETWEEN THE FINGERS

GENERAL GUIDELINES

Wide spacing between fingers shows many diverse interests in life (often found on the hands of extroverts).

Narrow spacing between fingers shows the focusing-in of the attention on specialised interests (often found on the hands of introverts).

When spacing is extreme there is a tendency to compartmentalise or "parcel-out" life experiences. Often either information or money slips easily through these people's hands.

Conversely where the fingers are tightly held together and curl in to the palm, great caution, obedience and a strict control of self-expression is indicated. In my experience such individuals are tense and wary of strangers; conditions brought about by traumatic experiences, hardships and stress. These people are often the "victim of circumstances". I am especially caring and sympathetic towards them – any form of criticism may cause distress.

THE SETTINGS OF THE FINGERS

As a general rule high set fingers show a sense of security and position with society. Low set fingers show insecurity and loss of esteem either personally or professionally.

INDEX FINGER

HIGH SET - Egotism, ambition, domination – "Hallmark of The Leader".

LOW SET - Lack of faith, hopelessness, loss of esteem – "The Victim".

MIDDLE FINGER

HIGH SET - Responsibility, duty, honour – "Conventional Respect".

LOW SET - Immorality, anarchy, loss of social position – "The Rebel".

THIRD FINGER

HIGH SET - Perfectionism, public service – "Creative Expression".

LOW SET - Gambling, lust – "The Fraud and Confidence Trickster".

FOURTH FINGER

HIGH SET - Charisma, sex appeal – "The Confident Communicator".

LOW SET – Inferiority, insecurity, naïveté – "Youthfulness".

FINGER TIP SHAPES

The finger tips express the way we communicate our ideas to others. In other words they represent the energy of self-expression.

FINGER TIP SHAPES

The finger tips express the way we communicate our ideas to others.
In other words the represent the energy of self-expression.

Square/Practical Tip

Cautious, shy, reserved in the use of spoken or written words. Traditional, methodical, conventional and obedient in public or private situations.

Intellectual/Philosophical Tip

Reasoning, discrimination, thoughtful, possessing mental dexterity, often taking enjoyment in debating. Development of strong psychological or philosophical beliefs in their personal and public lives.

Conic/EmotionalTip

Focused, inspired, sensitive, receptive to use of language. Spiritual, intuitive, refined and graceful in public and private life.

Spatulate/Energetic Tip

Aspiring, visionary, dynamic, fervent in their use of language. Idealistic, ardent, sometimes fanatical in their views, preferring action to words.

CHIROLOGY

i)   <u>MAJOR LINES OF THE PALM</u> (Refer to Figure Two)

Lines on the hand indicate a person's use of energy, being a representation of an individual's conscious and unconscious drives, mental and emotional attributes. There are four major lines being the MENTAL LINE, the EMOTIVE LINE, the LINE OF VITALITY and the CREATIVE LINE. The following is a table of attributes:

LINE FORMATION	RULERSHIP	ATTRIBUTES
LINE OF VITALITY (The Life Line)	SATURN	Representing the vital energy of the individual, their health, sustaining faculty, physical power and consciousness of TIME
LINE OF EMOTIONS (The Heart Line)	MOON	Representing intensity, feelings, emotions, intuition, circulatory system and consciousness of CHANGE
LINE OF MENTALITY (The Head Line)	MERCURY	Representing aspirations, discrimination, intellectual abilities and reasoning faculties, plus SELF-AWARENESS.
LINE OF CREATIVITY (Apollo)	SUN	Representing stability, self-assertion, ego, the arts and crafts, the metabolism of a person and consciousness of quality in THE FIVE SENSES

Vitality Line   = SOLID   - FOUNDATION   - Physical World

Emotional Line = FLUID   - ADAPTATION   - Intuitive World

Mental Line   = GASEOUS   - AWARENESS   - Communicative World

Creative Line   = ATOMIC   - EVOLUTIONARY   - Energetic World

LINE OF VITALITY (LIFE LINE)

This line encompasses the area of the mount of Venus, commencing under the Mount of Jupiter and above the area termed Lower Mars. It represents one's external vitality. The Line of mercury governs a person's Internal Metabolism.

A common mistake among students is to consider that a broken Life Line or short one indicates a short or unhealthy life. That is not true. In most cases a line will join with the Fate Line indicating a major change in lifestyle such as emigration, a career move or sometimes a marriage. It is only when the Inner Life of Mars (running inside the Life Line parallel to it) is broken that chronic illness is indicated. A well placed line is not tied to any other but gently curves round the palm to end below the Mount of Venus. It should give space to the Mount. Herein it indicates an expansive and generous nature, an optimist who will have many spheres of interest; these may be indicated by the size and quality of the Mount of Venus.

A line tied to the Head Line for 1 inch before the Life Line leaves it is an indication that a person's childhood may have been dominated by parental interference; when set low onto the Mount of Lower Mars courage has been sought.

A line commencing high on Jupiter or sending a Line to Jupiter illustrates a person's ambitions.

A line that breaks and has a parallel line which continues on course shows that a person has taken on a completely different lifestyle. Stress Lines may cut across the Vitality Line laterally at intervals; these are caused by people or events that affect a person's life.

The line will continue until the Mount of Neptune; here it may branch or be crossed by the Health Line. A line branching towards Luna indicates a person who is restless and may travel or emigrate (look for travel lines on Luna). When curving under the Mount of Venus a person will love their home and probably die in the country to which they are born.

Terminations in the Vitality Line vary. A tasselled end means a dissipation of life. It is quite common for the Line of Mercury to cross the Life Line. This indicates internal ailments. Chronology relating to this line will be shown in the latter part of this course. Note, if a person's Life line is close-held to the Mount of Venus, this indicates a cautious nature; possibly a narrow minded person or one who sacrifices much for one cause. A reserved, shy or frugal nature is often shown.

Finally, it is important to remember that the Vitality Line is linked metaphorically to all other major lines and reflects these lines.

LINE OF EMOTIONS (HEART LINE)

This line crosses the palm underneath the fingers, starting at the edge of the hand under the Mount of Mercury. The line represents a person's emotional response to life.

A balance person's line will flow across the hand terminating between the ringers of Jupiter and Apollo. This line shows a harmonious nature and a practical and caring response to others.

The HIGH SET HEART LINE indicates one who is demonstrative in their relationships. They will shout, scream, passionately debate and are sensual in their love-making.

The LOW SET HEART LINE indicates the opposite, namely one who is undemonstrative and represses their emotions. They will pout, moan and sulk, being calm, cool and rational, with a mental response to love-making.

In partnership matter similar Heart Lines show compatibility.

Often a Line also flows on to the Mount of Jupiter. This shows idealism and is often found on the hands of humanitarians, being a sign of philanthropy. These people love fervently and with generosity.

When a line descends and touches or joins the Vitality Line this is a sign of compassion, a life of sacrifice or a person relying on courage to maintain stability (this person will hide their emotions).

Lines rising onto Mercury are called Sympathy Lines or Medical Stigmata. They indicate great compassion and are vocational lines, e.g. counsellors, healers, therapists, doctors, nurses or vets.

Often people have a Girdle of Venus; this indicated added intensity of emotions, sensitivity, sensuality, dreams and fantasies – a secret world.

Dots on the Heart Line often indicate heart attacks and islands show respiratory problems. In general, from a health perspective, the Heart Line relates to the circulatory system.

LINE OF MENTALITY (HEAD LINE)

This line crosses the palm, commencing under the thumb and below the Mount of Jupiter and ending at some point on the Mount of Luna, parallel to the Line of Emotions. This line represents our thoughts and reasoning power and mental approach to life – discrimination.

It is often tied to the Life Lines; herein it shows a person sensitive to the needs of their family – a period of dependency. One is influenced by a third party, often parents or teachers.

When the line runs straight across the palm this indicates a practical and objective mentality – this is called the HIGH SET HEAD LINE. This person will be logical, reasoning, pragmatic or scientific. A long Line shows psychological understanding. The mentality rules over the emotions.

A line which sweeps down toward Luna is subjective; this person will probably be imaginative, artistic and intuitive – this is called the LOW SET HEAD LINE. The emotions rule over thinking.

A line descending to Lower Luna indicates a person with latent psychic ability. Conversely however this person may be a dreamer or at worst a manic depressive.

A line that forks at the end with one branch descending slightly has been called a Writers' Fork. "Imagination produces novels of worth". However painters or composers may also have this sign.

Lines that ascend towards the Line of Emotions indicate aspirations or mental gifts. Lines descending from this line indicate mental anxieties or the setback of a person's projects or careers.

The Line's attributes may be better understood when read in conjunction with the nail phalanges of the fingers, which represent mentality.

A long mental line shows a good memory, intelligence, perception, thoughtfulness, analytical, practical abilities – a person capable of organising and solving problems. When stretching to the edge of the palm, proficiency in psychology or exceptional mental dexterity may be present.

Short lines illustrate the impetuous, impulsive, active person, seeking challenges and experiences. Quick thinking, these people respond to energy situations fast and are instinctive in the execution of plans.

Very short lines (often found on Practical Hands) show a simplistic nature.

I have discovered that this line relates to the skeletal system so that where a line is broken a back problem is often indicated.

LINE OF CREATIVITY (THE APOLLO LINE)

This Line of Creativity may commence at any point on the lower palm but its destination is the Mount under the finger of Apollo. It represents a person's aspirations and is often related to careers. When the line commences on the Mount of Luna a career in the public eye is indicated, e.g. in service to the public (Civil Service, advertising, journalism).

When it commences from the Life Line or inside of it, this illustrates a person whose career is either self-made or influenced by the family.

The Line may not appear until above the Line of Emotions. Herein it represents hard work and achievement later in life, possibly through an interest.

A series of line underneath Apollo indicate versatility and a person's social standing. They will never be without friends or money for they are capable of adapting to various conditions.

A line terminated towards Mercury indicates a flair for business; when found towards Saturn the person has a great sense of responsibility and duty towards their work, e.g. a company man or devoted secretary.

A line commencing in the Higher Region of Luna, on the Percussion, and curving towards Apollo is a sign of business intuition; money will be easily generated and such a person may inherit wealth.

When the line is absent this indicates a perfectionist, never satisfied with their achievements.

THE LINE OF HEALTH (INTERNAL MEDICAL LINE)

The Health Line represents the internal health of a person and is the mirror of the Life Line which represented external health.

When absent the Health Line shows unusually robust health. Equally, a straight unbroken line shows good health. Broken lines show delicacy in health matters.

Where the line cuts into the Life Line it shows the need to look after one's health, being an indicator of dysfunction in the internal organs.

Like most Lines, the Life Line has "protector lines" providing support. Only when the Inner Line of Mars (turning parallel to the Life Line, but inside it) is broken is chronic ill-health shown.

Islands in this line show periods of ill-health. Dots in the Line show traumas or shocks. It is important to remember that the Health Line is <u>only one</u> of the indicators in health matters.

<u>THE LINE OF STABILITY</u> (THE FATE LINE)

The Fate Line, as it is traditionally termed, indicates the manifestation of the will to provide a direction in life. So we are talking about a person's identity; sense of worth, feelings of security and stability and their progress through life.

A well formed line commencing on the Mount of Neptune proceeding up the palm unbroken and deep is a sure sign of success in the career. I call this the "Vocational Line" because these people have a sense of dedication and purpose.

When commencing from within the Life Line, family influence in the choice of working life is shown. Proceeding from the Life Line itself is often the sign of the self-made careerist. Beginning from the Mount of Luna is an excellent position for anyone serving the public, indicating that success depends upon diplomacy. Often those in the public eye, especially actors and creative people, have this line feature.

Breaks in the line show career changes. If the line is made up of many small lines this is a sign of great instability both personally and professionally, being found on the hands of those who frequently change jobs as well as being the hallmark of the gambler and risk-taker!

The Fate Line is the barometer of change and therefore has great significance when dealing with health matters. It also is an ideal Line on which to judge the timing of events (CHRONOLOGY), e.g. when you move house. We will deal with these matters separately in later chapters.

FIGURE TWO: MAJOR LINES OF THE PALM

A - Life Line   B - Heart Line
C - Head Line   D - Line of Creativity
E - Health Line   F - Fate Line
G - Partnership Line   H - Children

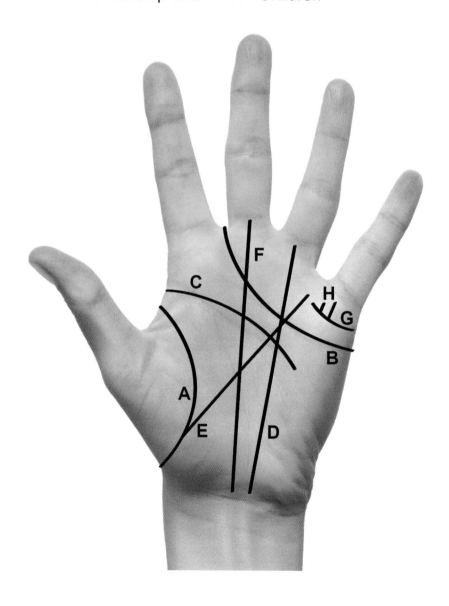

MINOR LINES OF THE PALM (refer to figure Three)

VIA LASCIVIA

This encompasses the Area of Neptune, from Luna to Venus, at the base of the palm. This line reflects the Ring of Venus and relates to not emotional but physical sensitivity.

Alcohol, drugs and risks should be avoided by the owner of this line. It represents sensitivity, allergies, anorexia, hypochondria or addictions.

THE GIRDLE OF VENUS (METABOLIC, EMOTIONAL HEALTH LINE)

When well formed, this indicates a psychologically well-balanced person, sensitive with deep emotions.

When broken it indicates intensity, dreams, fantasies and dramatic tendencies, e.g. role-playing.

Where one section of this Line from the base of the Finger of Apollo detaches itself and travels through the Heart and Head Lines touching the Life Line, this is one of the indicators of bisexuality or homosexuality. In this aspect fantasy has been transformed into real life! It is important as a palmist to be sensitive to people's rights as human beings to choose their own sexual orientation. This is why I have decided in this edition to rename the Marriage Line as the Partnership Line to reflect these individual preferences.

If the lines are stretched across the hand towards the Partnership Line, often suspicion or jealousy are present.

RING OF SOLOMON

This sign is indicated by a curved line underneath the index finger. This illustrates a person who prefers to work in a group. It may also show a person who is interested in learning.

A HIGH SET RING shows intuitive psychic abilities or an interest in the occult or philosophy.

A MIDDLE SET RING shows an understanding of psychology and often accompanies insight.

A LOW SET RING shows insight into practical matters, e.g. crafts.

When present on both hands, the ability to teach or train others will be present, especially where there is a Teachers' Square on the Mount of Jupiter.

Ring of Saturn

This encompasses the Mount of Saturn. This indicates a stern nature, serious, fatalistic, making the person reserved, cool and calculating.

Partnership Lines

This appears as a horizontal line or lines under the finger of Mercury. When straight it indicates a harmonious love life.

When curved downwards it indicates disappointments in love or that the loving partner may die before you do! When forked at the end a separation or divorce is a possibility.

Lines rising vertically from this line show children. Thin lines indicate girl children and thick lines boys. Crosses on these lines show accidents to children.

SPECIAL NOTE: To interpret this Line accurately we should be aware of two very important factors. Firstly, the Line is principally concerned with love and affection. However I have met single people, elderly ladies and many other people who have possessed this Line but never married. Some of these people love animals, e.g. a cat or dog, adopt children or in other ways express affection. So it is true to say that in reality the line represents the object of one's affections.

Secondly, the number of Lines appearing on the palm is no certain indicator of partnership. I have three on my own hand but remain single, although I remain optimistic that one day I will find love and happiness. Love is the most important thing in life, without which fulfilment may be elusive.

The Quality of Lines

Lines may end in a number of ways. If they simply fade out, this shows a person's energy in that field, e.g. Mentality or Emotionality, has come to its natural end. Crosses indicate accidents and stars indicate a violent dispersal of energy.

A line ending with an island shows that confusion and frustration are present. Dots show shocks – on Head Line mental trauma; on the Heart Line, emotional upsets or heart attacks.

Note figures relating to line endings.

FIGURE THREE: MINOR LINES OF THE PALM

A - Bar Lines
C - Vertical Lines
E - Teacher's Square
G - Via Lascivia
I - Girdle of Venus

B - Hyper Striations
D - Medical Stigmata
F - Line of Intuition
H - The Ring of Solomon

FIGURE FOUR: CHRONOLOGY

The palm can be dated by using a number of references. These are
better illustrated pictorially. In general, lines reflect one another, and
therefore it is important to notice and look at the Major Lines and notice
that when events occue they are mirrored in other lines.

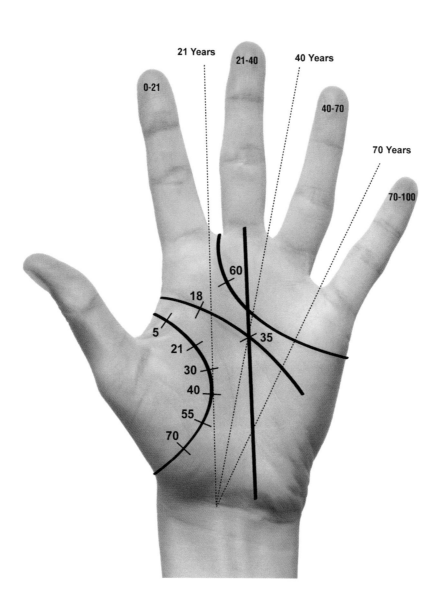

<u>SKIN RIDGE PATTERNS</u>

This area of study is called DERMATOGLYPHICS. Most people these days have heard of the Ancient Egyptians and the depictions of their lives visually and symbolically in the Pyramids.

Skin Ridge Patterns are the blue-prints (like a photographic negative) of the hands. Genetically people in family groups who are blood related will have similar finger print patterns.

The Palmar Skin Ridge Patterns show personality and social indicators. The Finger Print Patterns show psychological orientation. Please now refer to the Skin Ridge Diagram below which shows the position and meanings of these patterns.

<u>FINGER PRINT PATTERNS</u>

FINGER TIP PATTERNS

Practical Print Pattern - *Simple Arches*
Practical, methodical and instinctive, these people serve us, physically or socially, eg. craftsmen, social workers.

Energetic Print Pattern - *Extended Arches*
Enthusiastic, vibrant, idealistic, possessing 'nervous energy', and acting instinctively.

Emotional Print Pattern - *Loops*
Responsive, adaptable and sociable, these people are good at empathising both personally and professionally

Mental Print Pattern - *Concentric Circles*
Clever, original, independent, individualistic and seeking to be 'in control', eg. self employed.

FIGURE FIVE: DERMATOGLYPHICS
Skin Ridge Patterns

A - Raja Loop *(Public Service)*   B - Loop of Serious Intent
C - Loop of Humour   D - Line of Courage
E - Loop of Reason   F - Loop of Nature
G - Psychic Abilities   H - Loop of Vision
I - Loop of Instinct   J - Loop of Music *(The Bee-sting)*

SKIN TYPES

There are four basic skin types. An interesting fact is that people can, for instance, have a Conic or Emotional hand type but have the Energetic skin type. With skin we are concerned with the quality of life, experiences and specifically relationships.

ENERGETIC SKIN TYPE -FIRE

Energetic skin type is fairly coarse. It has wide pores and indicates response of life of an active kind. It has been, in my experience, likely that at least two finger print patterns will also have Whorl formations

EMOTIONAL SKIN TYPE- WATER

Emotional skin type is extremely fine and silky and has small pores. This indicates a person who will have a sensitive response to life. Memory may be good and there is a strong possibility that the person will have many thin lines on the hand.

INTELLECTUAL SKIN TYPE- AIR

Intellectual skin type is also fine skin, but the hand will probably be more rounded and plump. There will be fewer lines on the palm and the person will have a mental response to life.

PRACTICAL SKIN TYPE –EARTH

Practical skin type is very coarse and thick. A person with this skin has a potentially practical approach to life. There may be few lines. The hand may also have calluses and rough knuckle formations.

THE MOUNTS OF THE PALM

Mounts on the palm are reservoirs of energy. They represent quality and are found underneath the digits and at the side of the palm.

The following Major Mounts appear on the palm – Venus, Jupiter, Saturn, Apollo, Mercury, Luna; and in addition Minor Mounts – Upper Mars, Lower Mars, Neptune.

There is an apice in the centre of each Mount which forms a tri-radius of lines around it. Mounts may be central or displaced.

MOUNT OF JUPITER

When centrally placed this Mount represents dignity, self-respect and moral convictions. When displaced towards Saturn a persons' duty to family or society is shown. Displacement towards the thumb indicates a lack of caution, an adventurous nature, but one inclined towards delinquency or recklessness.

MOUNT OF SATURN

When centrally placed the Mount indicates common-sense and a good understanding of financial values. Displaced towards Apollo indicates a lack of caution in dealing with money. When the Mount is low set an interest in land-owning is shown.

MOUNT OF APOLLO

A well place Mount is a good sign for the practical artist who will show instinctive creative expression. When looped towards the Line of Emotions it indicates a compassionate nature and one who may love animals or small children.

MOUNT OF MERCURY

A person with a centrally placed apice will have a love of words: verbal expression or literature. Such a person may simply like crossword puzzles or enjoy reading historical biographies. When it leans towards Apollo, a person may be gifted with words, e.g. a writer.

MOUNT OF VENUS

The Mount of Venus represents harmony, a sense of beauty and physical passion. When high set it shows a well adapted sense of love. Over-full shows voluptuousness, whilst under-developed shows coldness. Apices on hands are rare and show collective memory and strong ties between religion and the person – a code of living.

MOUNT OF NEPTUNE

The Mount symbolises the Earth and relates to unconscious desires and a persons' psyche. A well developed Mount may indicate awareness and good memory with an active subconscious mind.

MOUNT OF LUNA

An apex here indicates a selfless worker for who recognition does not come. The Mount represents the subconscious and imaginative side of a persons' nature. When this area is rounded, a gift of Spiritual Healing may be apparent (The Creative Curve).

FIGURE SIX: THE MOUNTS

The Mounts	Talents
A - Mount of Mercury	Speech, Singing, Linguistics
B - Mount of Apollo	Arts, Crafts, Management
C - Mount of Saturn	Science, Skills, Administration
D - Mount of Jupiter	Power, Religion, Politics
E - Lower Mars	Courage, Gambling
F - Mount of Venus	Love, Passion, Music
G - Mount of Neptune	Subconscious talents
H - Mount of Luna	Imagination
I - Upper Mars	Inner strength
J - Mount of Mars	Area of life activity

LOVE AND SEXUALITY IN THE HANDS

Like Astrology, Palmistry can be used to interpret in a compatibility system similar to Synastry to determine Hand-Chart harmonies.

HAND-TYPE MATCHING CHARACTERISTICS

A.   Square/Practical Hands

LOVE – Traditional family value predominate. Finding a capable, down to earth partner, getting married, having children, is of paramount importance. Stability, security and support are vital.

SEXUALITY – Sensual, hedonistic, strong physical lust and stamina combine with caution, distrust of words and undemonstrative love. Loyalty, trust and devotion are demanded.

B.   Conical/Emotional Hands

LOVE – Sympathetic, compassionate, caring values where emotions are easily expressed and desired. Intuitive and spiritual, physical beauty or shared ideals are essential. Fertile, loving and unselfish, positive and negative emotions can join.

SEXUALITY – Flexible, nubile, imaginative, soft and tactile, relaxed, steamy. Prolonged love making is preferred.

C.   Philosophical/Mental Hands

LOVE – Partnerships, shared beliefs, humour and exciting locations. Express versatility and intellectual agreement. Role-playing and creativity make for stimulating, flexible relationships.

SEXUALITY – Inventive, dramatic, imaginative, love-making may be like a game of physical chess or in an unusual location e.g. the "mile high club".

D.   Energetic/Spatulate Hands

LOVE – Impulsive, intense, enthusiastic love-making, which combine physical and intellectual needs. Active, aggressive, love is conquest, an ecstatic battle.

SEXUALITY – Passionate, sensuous, sex is quick and energetic, fast and impetuous. Anytime, anyway, anyhow, we want it now!

COMPATIBLITY

Square/Practical	Square/Practical	Harmonious	Compatible
Square/Practical	Conic/Emotional	Harmonious	Compatible
Square/Practical	Spatulate/Energetic	Antagonistic	Incompatible
Square/Practical	Spatulate/Energetic	Antagonistic	Incompatible
Conic/Emotional	Square/Practical	Harmonious	Compatible
Conic/Emotional	Conic/Emotional	Harmonious	Compatible
Conic/Emotional	Philosophical/Mental	Antagonistic	Incompatible
Conic/Emotional	Spatulate/Energetic	Antagonistic	Incompatible
Philosophical/Mental	Square/Practical	Antagonistic	Incompatible
Philosophical/Mental	Conic/Emotional	Antagonistic	Incompatible
Philosophical/Mental	Philosophical/Mental	Harmonious	Compatible
Philosophical/Mental	Spatulate/Energetic	Harmonious	Compatible
Spatulate/Energetic	Square/Practical	Antagonistic	Incompatible
Spatulate/Energetic	Conic/Emotional	Antagonistic	Incompatible
Spatulate/Energetic	Philosophical/Mental	Harmonious	Compatible
Spatulate/Energetic	Spatulate/Energetic	Harmonious	Compatible

As in Astrology, people may be attracted to their opposite. Also the myriad of palmar features should be considered to determine compatibility, especially the Heart Lines.

IN DEPTH ANALYSIS

Like in Astrology, where not only the Zodiac Sign but all of the birth charts are compared, so in Palmistry we look at the fingers and thumbs, skin ridge patterns, the Mounts, major and minor lines to determine definite positive and negative traits.

However as this is rather complex these matters will be give space in my Professional Palmist's Teaching Manual to be published later in 1995.

Meanwhile why not try creating your own hand charts as a reference tool?

EQUIPMENT FOR THE PALMIST

A large magnifying glass is essential to read palmar features in detail, as is a ruler to measure hand shapes, dimensions of the fingers and major lines. It is invaluable when measuring the Fate Line to determine the timing of events.

GLOSSARY OF TERMS

TERMS

Chirology	- the analytical study of hands
Chirognomy	- the study of the shape of the hands
Chiromancy	- the study of the Palmar Region
Hermetic	- appertaining to the Ancient Philosophy of Creation
Karma	- the Laws of Cause and Effect
Macrocosm	- Mankind observed as a component manifestation of Divine Consciousness
Microcosm	- the manifestation in human consciousness of external cosmic phenomena
Ontology	- the study of the essence of being
Palmistry	- the art of Hand Divination – fortune telling

OTHER MISCELLANEOUS LINES

- islands indicate disillusionment

- bars and dots indicate barriers and shocks

- tassels indicate dissipation of energy

- wavy lines show vacillation

- vertical lines show activity

- horizontal lines show inhibitions

- curved lines within the Life Line are influence lines,

   being parents or loved ones reinforcing a person's energy

MISCELLANEOUS PALMAR FEATURES

Islands		- periods of confusion or disillusionment
Dots		- shocks/traumas either physical or psychological
Wavy Lines		- vacillation, indecision, procrastination, hesitancy
Crosses		- setbacks
Stars		- violence, great trauma, e.g. nervous breakdowns
Squares		- protection, safety, preservation from harm
Triangles		- good fortune, success
Forks		- division of energies or separation e.g. divorce
Breaks		- change of direction for good or ill
Bars		- inhibitions, restraints, blocks
Grilles		- struggle, lack of progress

FEATURES ON FINGERS AND THEIR PHALANGES

Striations (vertical lines) | | | - talents, skills, abilities

Hyper-Striations (many Striations) |||||| - stress, overwork

Bars   ===   - inhibitions, blocks to achievement

MEANINGS OF FINGER PHALANGES

Base Phalanges   - practical, down-to-earth skills and abilities

Middle Phalanges   -executive, organisation, management skills

Top Phalanges   - mental or spiritual abilities e.g.
politics/clairvoyance

SUGGESTED RECOMMENDED BOOKS TO READ

* = Good : ** = Important : *** = Excellent (the best!)

A.   Any books by Chiro, the famous Palmist   *

B.   Annals of Human Genetics by Sir Francis Galton (EUGENICS)
      **

C.   The Human Hand, the Living Symbol of Noel Jacquin
      ***

D.   Hands and Faces by Mrs Katherine Ashton   *

E.   The Science of Hand Reading Simplified by K.C. Sen
      **

F.   No-Nonsense Hand Reading by Rev. T. Dukes
      **

G.   The Hand in Psychological Diagnosis by C. Wolfe
      ***

H.   The Human Hand by Sir Charles Bell
      ***

I.   Laws of Scientific Hand Reading by W. Benham
      ***

J.   The Palmistry Work-Book by Nathaniel Altman
      ***

K.   Chinese Hand Analysis by Shifu T. Dukes
      ***

L.   The Theory of Metaphysical Influence by N. Jacquin
      ***

M.   Studies in Hand Readings by N. Jacquin
      **

N.   How to Read Hands by Lori Reid

Many excellent books are out of print. Seek out a good specialist second hand book shop.

John Harrison is the Founder of The Association of Palmistry Counsellors.

YOUR FIRST PALMISTRY READING

Ok, so now is the time to put knowledge into practice. Choose a friend or someone you feel comfortable with and try to make this a "fun exercise", a light hearted experience.

SETTING THE SCENE

Relax. Do some meditation. Clear your personal thoughts and concentrate on the other person sending them thoughts of sympathy and understanding.

Sit in a well lit room that is warm and pleasant. Light a candle, play soft music or light incense if you are both happy with this. We are trying to create an ambience and a welcoming atmosphere.

LET'S GO FOR IT!

Gently take both of your friend's hands in yours. Close your eyes and use your intuition. How is this person feeling now?

After a few moments open your eyes and spend 3-5 minutes looking at their hands. Notice the shape of their hands, the Major and Minor lines. Take up your magnifying glass and closely inspect the finger print patterns. Look at the Mounts and finally the skin ridge patterns.

Think simple thoughts, e.g. are these large or small hands? Are they smooth or rough to the touch? Are there few lines or many lines? Are the fingers long or short, wide spread or close held? Are the lines strong and unbroken or thin and fragile? Are the finger prints all the same type or different? Now feel the Mounts and decide which are the best developed; these will show social skills. Are the Mounts fleshy or flat and hard? Are there any skin ridge symbols on these hands, e.g. Loop of Humour or Loop of Seriousness?

BEGINNING YOUR READING – Feeling nervous? Me too!!!

So the first thing to decide upon is the hand shape. Start by asking yourself whether the fingers are long or short relative to the length of the palm. If short, your friend has either Practical or Spatulate hands; if long, either Conic or Intellectual hands. The difference between the two types of short fingered hands is that the Practical hand is square, e.g. just as long as it is wide. The difference between the Conic and Intellectual hand is that the Conic hand is narrow or thin with long tapering fingers. Refer to your notes and state the indication for the hand type.

Now look at the fingers and thumbs. Pay special attention at the proportions of these e.g. long, short, thick or thin. We now need to look at the finger prints which will give a unique insight into the mind of our friend e.g. sociable, idealistic, individualistic, enthusiastic and energetic, imaginative. Make your interpretation of the thumb followed by each finger in succession. Longer fingers and thumbs show a greater range of ability. Shorter ones show limits to ability.

Next we come to the palm itself and the lines. Begin with the Life Line. If long and unbroken this will show an active life with an expectance of 75 or more. A short or broken line shows change and the need to take care of the health.

The Head Line is now analysed. Long or short, straight (high set) or curved (low set). Refer to your notes.

The Heart Line follows this. Long, ending between the Index and Second fingers? They are demonstrative with affections and emotionally responsive. Short or lower set? They are practical, independent and self-reliant.

The Fate line – a long unbroken line shows an excellent career. Where broken, changes are apparent.

Now after looking at the Health line, proceed to look at all the Minor lines, e.g. partnerships, Girdle of Venus, Ring of Solomon etc.

Lastly we look at the skin ridge patterns to gauge individual personality traits.

SUMMARY

In the process of your reading you will have begun with looking at both hands together. Then you would have looked exclusively at the left hand which represents development since childhood and moved on to the right hand which shows growth of aptitudes and beliefs. You will notice differences. In practice this means that your friend is changing and evolving as a person!

You are now in a position to summarise your findings.

A WORD ABOUT HONESTY

Honesty is important. Telling the truth is important. Do you know the truth? Remember that every human being is fallible and only God knows everything. For this reason be diplomatic and humble. Your words can heal or destroy. Choose them carefully. Both the hands are the lines upon them are in a constant state of change and like life itself, unpredictable. Give encouragement, support and a positive approach. Never mention death or strong negative statements. Allow your friend to ask questions. Try to answer these honestly. Thank and bless them for the privilege of allowing you into their life.

TIME TO TEST YOURSELF

Here's your opportunity to examine your new found skills and learning. Let's imagine that Mary-Jo and Pedro Gonzalez are two of your friends and they have come to you for a reading!

TEST Write or tape-record your findings as if it were a real consultation. How do you perceive these people? What are their strengths and weaknesses? How could you help them? Next, refer to your notes to check your knowledge. Don't worry if you've made mistakes – we all do! What have you learnt?

MARY-JO'S HANDS

Hand Shape	She has a square palm and short fingers
Skin Ridge Patterns loop	She has a whorl print pattern on her index fingers. On her palms, a appears between the third and fourth fingers
Spacing/Setting	Her fingers are all wide spaced. Her little fingers are low set
Major Lines	Her Head line is low set. Her Heart line is high set
Minor lines	She possesses Medical Stigmata and Via Lascivia
Finger Phalanges	All Mary's lower base phalanges are well developed and full

ANSWERS:

Mary-Jo's **square hands** indicate she is practical, strong, reliable and methodical. **Whorl finger prints** would point towards independence and self-reliance with the **Loop of Humour** showing her to be witty and fun loving.

The **wide spacing** of the fingers shows her to be extrovert with many interests. Her little finger shows insecurity and naïveté, but does indicate she gets on well with children.

As regards the **Major Lines**, the **Head Line** indicates someone who is imaginative and perceptive, although her heart rules her head. The **Heart Line** indicates she is demonstrative in affections.

With the **Minor Lines**, the presence of **Medial Stigmata** would indicate an ability in counselling, healing or therapies. The **Via Lascivia** would point towards metabolic sensitivity e.g. allergies, hypochondria or addictions to say coffee, alcohol or cigarettes.

The **Phalanges** show that Mary enjoys material comforts, e.g. food, drink, luxuries, possessions, sex, etc.

Mary-Jo is an Occupational Therapist specialising in paediatrics in a Senior Management position.

PEDRO GONZALEZ' HANDS

Hand Shape	He has a square palm and long, rounded fingers
Skin Ridge Patterns	On the middle fingers he has the simple arch prints
Spacing/Setting	Pedro's fingers are wide spaced. His index finger is high low set
Major Lines	His Head line is long, in the high set position. His Heart line is in the low set position
Minor Lines	He has the Girdle of Venus well formed and the Ring of Solomon (medium set) with the Teachers' Square
Finger Phalanges	All his lower base phalanges are well developed and full

ANSWERS:

Pedro Gonzalez' hand shape would indicate he is intellectual, discriminating and possessing good reasoning powers. **Simple Arch finger prints** would point towards practical abilities at work, e.g. crafts, machinery or social skills.

The **wide spacing** of the fingers shows him to be extrovert with wide interests and the **Setting** of the index finger shows him to be assertive and confident possibly even domineering.

As regards the **Major Lines,** the **Head Line** indicates Pedro is rational, logical, equipped with excellent analytical skills or psychological insights. The **Heart Line** indicates he is undemonstrative in love, i.e. he mentalises his feelings.

With the **Minor Lines**, the presence of **Girdle of Venus** indicates underlying strong, powerful emotions which are being repressed, as well as dreams, fantasies and role-playing skills. The **Ring of Solomon** shows he has intuitive gifts (psychological abilities) and the **Teachers' Square** would indicate an ability to teach.

Pedro is a Psychotherapist. He teaches remedial craft skills at a hospital.

SMILE HOLISTIC PRACTICE

MEDITATION CLASSES

(relax, feel peace, discover the real you!)

REIKI HEALING COURSE/TREATMENTS

(rejuvenate, re-energise, learn to heal yourself and others)

THOUGHT FIELD THERAPY

(relief from phobias, traumas, addiction and grief)

PALMISTRY COUNSELLING

(guidance on health, careers, relationships, private readings,

party bookings, tuition and lectures)

MR JOHN HARRISON – I.T.E.C., PALMISTRY COUNSELLOR

Telephone: 01773-688479

E-mail: smile4u@yahoo2024.co.uk

Websites: http://john-harrison-palmistry.com

http://smileholistictherapies.com , http://meditation-4u2.com

*Postal Tuition Courses *Reading by email *Talks *Workshops*

*Events *Private Consultation *Party Bookings

With thanks to contributors

Images by http://www.scottgaunt.co.uk

Compiled by http://homebusinesszone.co.uk

Made in the USA
Charleston, SC
03 April 2015